Spirited Sonnets

Poems by
Christine Burrows

Front cover:

**Created with two superimposed
photographs taken by the Author**

Another Wonderful Day

At break of day when rising with the sun—
appreciation fills hearts with desire.
To start my day, an energetic run—
will set the pace, as birds sing in the choir.

The freshness in the air will fill my lungs
I'm breathing in the smells of nature's toil,
the perfumes and the fruitful smell of plums—
aromas of a cultivated soil.

I never tire of living in the centre—
and welcome light from nature's brand new day;
the early bee, collecting sweetened nectar—
so earnestly all creatures come to play.

I'm grateful for the time I spend on earth,
such rich abundant pleasures I observe.

Dedication:

I dedicate this book to:

Lucinda Rose Jobson

This girl has a free spirit
and adores poetry

Author's Preface:

Sonnets have been a passion of mine since I first read Shakespeare's sonnets at school. I admire the form, the melody of iambic pentameter and the sentiment a sonnet delivers to the reader. The turn of events in the third stanza adds an alternative view point with a touch of wisdom in the final couplet to complete the picture. The sonnets within refer to modern day events, and cover a wide range of subjects, from love and loss, nature, human emotions and world affairs from my own personal perspective. I am sure you will identify with my words, and I hope these sonnets serve to soothe, disturb, confirm beliefs, challenge ideas, educate the reader, and also entertain. There is a sonnet here for everyone.

A sonnet is a 14 line poem, usually consisting of 10 syllables per line and written in iambic pentameter which means the stress of a word is on the second syllable. The end rhymes usually follow an ABAB rhyme scheme. The metre gives the sonnet its distinctive melody. The Volta is a changing thought process written into the third stanza, followed by a two line couplet to complete the story.

We can thank the Italians for the original sonnet, it is reported to have been invented in the thirteenth century by *Giancomo da Lentinie* and later modified by humanist and scholar *Francesco Petrarch. Sir Thomas Wyatt* and *Henry Howard* introduced it into England in the 16th century and *William Shakespeare* published his book of sonnets in 1609, modifying the sonnet into a Shakespearean Sonnet as we know it today.

Life leaves its scar on our heart, and rocks our spirit. We all leave our footprint behind no matter how insignificant we think it is, we are all making history in our own back yard In all cultures, emotions are universally recognised, no matter who we are, we all have the same basic feelings. We have regrets, triumphs and lasting memories. We are individuals with opinions. To be human is to err. We make a difference, even when we stumble.

Poetry not only records life, it identifies situations we face. Poetry makes us feel less alone as we are in this life together and face the same, or similar challenges every day. Rhyming words are powerful and can soothe the soul, lift the spirit, excite and infuse the reader with confidence and self-esteem. Poetry confirms our feelings in melodic words that help us come to terms with sorrow, and encourages us to keep the faith and continue to love. We hope to greet the sun every day with positivity, and if we keep love in our hearts, and believe in human nature, we will live a good life. These sonnets will reach inside your soul and hopefully touch your heart within, sing to you, and leave a lasting word to ponder.

Enjoy: " Spirited Sonnets"

Contents

When striding one step forward, two steps back
I wonder at my lack of concentration.
The track I've chosen may be out of whack
I cannot seem to reach my destination.

My panic seems to claw inside my mind
as thoughts can be unkind. I'm in distress
a sign that I am being left behind,
my journey now is weak and powerless.

It's all because I need to go to sleep.

A Bitter Word

A bitter word can leave a shard of glass—
so deep within, the scar may never heal;
as once released it is as bold as brass,
and leaves a feeling cold as rigid steel.

The menacing is riddled with a rot
corroding overtime, but never gone;
and what remains still hits a tender spot—
that very moment we still come upon.

The word delivered innocently bruised—
the speaker didn't give a second thought
to how it was received or it abused,
and now it resonates and won't abort.

A word lives on forever in the mind—
and wounds just like a sword when it's unkind.

A Life without Liberty

She never saw the light or felt the sun,
and early dreams were thwarted by her angst,
her memories would sully life to come—
she'd take without a single word of thanks.

Entitled was she by her own admission,
to keep command of others from her throne;
not every soul would give her their commission,
as some escaped to live life on their own.

At night she was still haunted by her ghosts,
tormented was she by her heavy burden;
determined to keep face with all her hosts
although the life she led behind a curtain . . .

was unfulfilled until her dying breath,
no liberty was felt until her death.

A Look

A message that's conveyed from eye to eye,
is classified and undisclosed to others,
and only the receiver will comply—
a look can be exhausting, as it smothers.

The power of a look can cut through glass
and touch without a word, without a sound;
as daggers can be felt and will harass
with splinters that will crush and be profound.

The eye can be a window to the soul,
when blind, no message hurts or can reflect,
so never glance at someone in control—
it's fear that they rely on to connect.

A dirty look can steal a person's zeal,
and undermine the happiness they feel.

A Solid Friendship

In you I see a heart that's young and gay,
and unaffected by the mounting years;
an open door with helpful words to say,
a place where I can shed my woeful tears.

Your ear will listen when my words spill out,
you never judge me or leave your critique,
and even if I want to scream and shout,
your warm advice is helpful and unique.

I gift to you this Sonnet for today,
as you deserve a wealth of goodly wishes;
enjoying celebrations here in May,
I send to you some hugs and heartfelt kisses.

I'm blessed to have a friend like you around,
as you keep both my feet on solid ground.

Happy Birthday Angela

A Night I won't Forget

The setting sun exuded tranquil hues,
my sparkly dress and shoes matched all the stars;
as dinner, show and bubbles can diffuse,
a night spent with the girls will soothe my scars.

An angry word was thrown in my direction,
I kept my cool, and calmed the mood with smiles;
but I did not expect this insurrection,
the alcohol had fuelled the aisles for miles.

And in a jealous rage her words would fly,
and stunned by this display, I had no words;
my only question would be why I try
to understand behaviour so absurd.

I kept my counsel and integrity
as alcohol kills with hostility.

Abuse of Power

Who kicks a man when he is truly down?
And speaks of hate, as if it were alright.
Who plunges knives in flesh to gain the crown?
The devil has an eagerness tonight.

The brutal, forceful wickedness is rife,
no one escapes the sword inside this castle;
and heads will roll, there goes another life,
a shadow cast, for someone else to dazzle.

But standing firm upon your strong foundations,
battle ready with your helmet on;
when scorn is thrown, deflect these situations—
calm and graceful, peaceful as a swan.

With empathy intact, we understand,
the yearn to be in charge, and in command.

And what is gained from stabbing in the back—
as littered is the path with old cadavers;
Macbeth soon learned his bloody cold attack
did not win hearts with fearful savage daggers.

A word, a deed, an active bow and arrow,
to pierce the heart of someone unawares,
will leave a trail of death, a dull dark shadow,
and disappoints the Man who lives upstairs.

Remember not to tread on other souls,
and dish the dirt in order to excel,
as everyone can reach desired goals,
without the need to send the rest to hell.

If you believe a rumour, let it feed,
then you abuse your power with your deed.

Age, a Blessing or a Curse

As age decays our bones, our mind is clear,
we steer our life with knowledge of the past,
experience has roots inside our fear,
we hope the stains will fade when die is cast.

Selectively we choose the safest path,
and know that grave mistakes will cost us dear,
we calculate the bitter aftermath
and save ourselves the trouble of a tear.

But some may say in old age we are fools,
and soon forget our name, and where we live;
the privilege of age means all those tools
are lost when cells deplete, we must forgive.

A wise man said, our faith in honesty—
will turn us into victims who agree.

Alcohol Rules

I sipped the nectar filled with toxic fizz,
and felt it blow my mind and slur my words,
and understanding others was a quiz
my vision blurred, the spinning room disturbs.

I can't stand up, my legs have turned to jelly,
my stomach churns and I might soon be sick;
the door keeps closing on me, it's too heavy,
I might pass out, I need to sit down— quick.

Now I have lost control, I am defenceless,
relying on some stranger for advice;
and nothing suits my mood, I am contentious,
behaving like a lout to be precise.

The nectar in my bloodstream rules my mind,
destroying who I am, I'm redefined.

An Omen

A single raven landed on my porch,
his well-dressed feathers formal, bold and black,
he danced upon the railings to report—
that it was time to give my guy the sack.

The boyfriend that I'd tolerated here,
was acting like a pompous childish cad;
and threatening to leave, it was quite clear—
it was the best solution, he was mad.

And when I saw the raven jump about,
I knew it was a sign to let him go,
he packed his bag and then I saw him out,
his temper reached a damaging plateau.

The end had come, a welcoming relief,
this omen had released me from my grief.

Another Unjust Conviction

They locked him up for seventeen long years
for crimes they since discovered were not his,
although his keen protesting brought some tears,
ignored was he by lawyers and by pigs.

And when they found him innocent and free
they charged him for his stay inside the prison!
In debt, he has to find the cash you see—
for board and lodgings, he owed them commission!

Is there no culpability today?
Now free, is he still persecuted here?
How can they make the innocent still pay—
some compensation qualifies, it's clear.

Injustice never fails to leave its tale,
recorded is another court room fail.

Andrew Malkinson, 57, was found guilty of raping a woman in Greater Manchester in 2003 and the following year he was jailed for life with a minimum term of seven years. He served 10 more because he maintained his innocence. His conviction was quashed after DNA evidence linking another man to the crime came to light.

Her Majesty's Prison Service want him to pay for board and lodgings and this will be taken from any compensation claim.

Arrogant Entitlement

Pretentiously, assumptions have no truth
the egotist will have a boastful swagger;
and vanity is not confined to youth—
self-righteous folk know how to draw the dagger.

And your demise gives wings to insolence—
a condescending tirade of deceit;
and now's the time to show intolerance,
when disapproving arrogance repeats.

If wounded by their words then picture this,
some sour with age and some with age may mellow
as some may live without a loving kiss—
and others wear a streak of sissy yellow.

So never give your time to pompous souls,
humility is absent from their bones.

As Gentle as a Grecian Sea

Oh, how unstable is my step when I
speak of your spirit bright as stars above;
and tongue-tied am I when I question why
you left so soon, but left behind your love.

And never will I walk without a cheer,
as I remember all you did for me;
your passion was as subtle as a tear—
and gentle as a Grecian summer sea.

I hear your quiet voice above the din,
your wise and calming gestures still impress;
and life continues when the violin
recants the life we lost, now acquiesce.

Your heart was always open, never blind;
and those who never met you, know you're kind.

Assumptions

We think we know, but much we have assumed,
and in that vague assumption we are blind;
as when a morbid thought has been exhumed—
it festers into views that are unkind.

How can we know the truth behind a screen,
no knowledge gave us rights to make them valid;
yet based on our opinion we are keen
to make assumptions that are mean and avid.

Step back and keep an open minded view,
we never know another's pain or joy;
we cannot know if skies are grey or blue
conjecture has a chance to just annoy.

Remember we don't have a crystal ball—
so don't assume that you can know it all!

Auguries of Fate

To hold the fate of someone in your hand,
the power to have mercy or to kill;
decisions are released from high command,
depending on a word inked from a quill.

To govern, offer clemency and grace
and empathise and understand another;
to give without reward, our warm embrace,
and not enslave our sister or our brother.

The benefits in life are on display,
and some are born to endless nights of pain;
when others bathe inside the light of day,
we never know when we will feel the rain.

Our fate's not guided by the moon and stars,
but often by those people leaving scars.

Balancing Life

I had a conversation with myself
and learned I am the harshest of all critics;
deciding that to keep in perfect health,
I need to work much harder than those cynics.

I know I can't be fooled by rich temptations,
and discipline is what I need to keep;
to own my failings and my limitations,
allow myself some time to get some sleep.

The joys of planning always reap rewards,
a minute won't be wasted when its shared;
and time must be productive as awards
are never won unless we are prepared.

Remember to allow time to relax,
as busy lives cause major heart attacks.

Battle Scars

A soldier knows too well the battle sounds,
where he walked hand in hand with death and fear;
and wears the scars upon his face— he frowns,
how many lives were lost without a tear.

A soldier sees his fellow men die young,
he witnesses realities of war;
inside he bears a broken hearted song,
that leaves the grief and sorrow at his core.

A soldier may survive, return back home,
where family will love and care for him;
but he cannot forget, he's left alone
with memories of horror and of sin.

Experiences cannot be undone,
in war survivors never think they've won.

Beasties

Those tiny creatures underground are busy,
they turn the earth, and excavate below;
as toiling everyday makes them all dizzy,
the ants, the beetles, worms and slugs are slow.

Inside the wood communities are thriving,
and silently these creatures are devout;
the bugs are having fun and some are jiving,
and dance among the flowers, fly about.

So if you see a bug, don't stamp on it!
Its mission is important, work won't stop.
So listen to the words, let bugs keep fit!
Let creepy crawlies frolic, jump and hop.

The park's alive with beasties on the ground,
tread carefully as they don't make a sound.

Behind Closed Doors

When outside looking in, the view is fine,
normality is oozing from the scene;
all smiles seem genuine, there is no crime,
a perfectly enacted smooth routine.

Within the house, a quiet calm appears,
and on the surface, everyone is free
to speak, converse and live without a tear,
a well-adjusted family is key.

But underneath the fake facade lies truth,
as plain as day, and everyone is fooled;
control and treachery is quite acute
no liberty exists, it's overruled.

Behind closed doors there lurks an evil seed,
and secretly they planted it to feed.

Binge Drinking

His bingeing started with a liquid lunch,
it stupefied his mind with alcohol;
this habit formed and soon became a crutch
and overtime collapse was visible.

He terrorised his family at night,
and bullied with a temper bold and brash,
his shameful nightly pattern would ignite—
destroying faith and peace within a flash.

Now all alone, there is no real regret—
his memory is numbed by constant drinking;
he lost his job, his wife, he is in debt,
now on the street, there is no room for thinking.

An early death would mute this trembling soul,
as drinking can destroy with its control.

Blame Game

When blame unjustly throws its bitter tongue,
and lashes at you like a poisoned snake;
consider whether you are right or wrong,
could claims be based on something false or fake?

Investigate the truth and it will show
that innocence has wings of liberty;
and fault will lie with others who will know
that guilty words can stain and cost a fee.

And some will blame you for their own wrongdoings,
when anger felt within has stained their soul;
remember not to leave your life in ruins,
when accusations wrongly take control.

The shame of lies in blaming other guys,
will leave a stain of guilt in people's eyes.

Bleeding Hearts

Can anger really cause a wound to bleed?
And spill the blood of someone not to blame,
when venom has the power to succeed--
it leaves an acrid smell within its shame.

In life we learn to navigate the arrows,
avoid an argument and quell the tide;
to dodge the bullet, duck beneath the gallows,
as life is precious, hearts retain the prize.

And I forgive those with a wilful thought,
and never let a spat destroy my world;
"they know not what they do", the bible taught,
I'm unconcerned, their words, remain unheard.

If anger spills and you become the target,
relax and ride upon your magic carpet.

Boastful Quotes

Who is it that says most, but knows so little?
Those boastful souls who loudly claim their fame;
and yet they have no impact, they are fickle,
and when explored there's nothing in their brain.

No dignity is left in those who boast,
there is no subtlety in vulgar words—
I think I'd rather make friends with a ghost,
than listen to some bragging that disturbs.

Give me a humble soul with gifted flair,
who lets the words upon the page speak out;
as those who blow their trumpet have no care
for others who are capable, devout.

So leave your swagger at the door my dear,
with you we know there's nothing here to fear.

Breathe in Life

The sun falls down, I rest my weary head,
the night is long, tomorrow may not come;
I sleep and hope that I may not be dead—
and dawn reminds me I am not yet done.

I praise the day and even if it rains
I feel the drops of moisture on my skin,
and if the sun begins to light the lanes,
then I am blessed with happiness within.

I breathe the air, enjoy a breakfast feast
how good it is to smile and walk a mile;
and as I've aged my yen for life increased,
I'm ready for the battle and the trial.

And in the afternoon my step, it slows,
my positivity for life reloads.

Bull Baiting Ring,

(Birmingham, B5 4BU)

When bulls are slaughtered in the ring of death
the blood will linger, seep into the roots;
a place where cattle took their final breath—
polluted air with carcasses of truth.

The centre where the tormenting took life,
for entertainment, dogs would run amok;
St Martins rang her bells to stop the strife
as crowds would gather, bloody scenes would shock.

A symbol of our wickedness within
now proudly represents a bygone time;
the bloody sport abhorrent and a sin—
the sacred bull reminds us of our crime.

In Birmingham where I was born and bred,
the shame hangs in the air just overhead.

During the 16th century a guy called John Cooper was given the right to bait bulls in the centre of Birmingham opposite St Martins Church, this became known as the Bull Ring.

Bull baiting is the practice of allowing dogs to torment bulls by biting them in an enclosed ring where there is no escape, to provide entertainment for the crowd.

The area around St. Martins by the 19th century, had become crowded with old buildings, narrow streets and traders stalls. Today the Bull Ring is a massive shopping centre and a bronze bull stands proudly at the entrance.

Bureaucrats

They hold the cards and never let you see,
as pushing pens on paper is their bag—
and keeping secrets under lock and key,
when in the system everything will drag.

No matter how frustrated you become,
the bureaucrats enjoy the time it takes
to throw a life line or a little crumb,
the information's coded if it breaks.

The documents required are stamped and sent,
the paperwork is churned out of the mill;
and reading it will let your temper vent,
in shock and horror at those words that chill.

The Government employs men to disrupt—
and most of them are sinful and corrupt.

Captured in a Song

The years have cruelly mounted since you left,
the summer of your days, a memory;
your calm and good advice I can't perfect,
your absence leaves an empty treasury.

I miss those thoughtful gestures every day,
the little things that made my life worthwhile;
appreciated more than words can say—
and captured in a song and in a smile.

The cherry tree forever stayed in mourning,
no blossoming, as seasons lost their plight;
as grief instilled a curfew with its stalling,
the days of Summer chilled with Winter's night.

The power of those songs that you adored,
bring comfort when I need to be restored.

Capturing Time

This time will age as 'now' becomes the past,
and captured in a word, these moments shine;
just like a photograph, the snap will last—
in poems, minutes stand the test of time.

Recorded on a page, the past still lives,
and generations learn about this thief;
it falls and slips away through cracks and sieves,
as harnessing our memory is brief.

But Shakespeare captured time within his sonnets,
he brought the word to us with verse and rhyme;
in times of old there were no electronics—
survival of his words defied all time.

My wish is that my word fulfils a purpose,
to capture life right now within this circus.

Careless Idioms

Unthrifty words can worm into the wood
and trees once tall and strong, diseased inside;
each letter lays a seed that is no good,
and soon the leaves turn brown and cannot hide.

The truth can topple influential men,
as rumour spreads and mobs take up their swords;
it started when the ink dripped from a pen
and marked a warrant with some new reforms.

The innocent lie dying on the ground,
the aftermath is bloodied with the dead;
and shame and deep regret without a sound
would permeate inside the writer's head.

A silent note has potent domination,
and changes scenes with cruel application.

Cheating Time

Refusing to be beaten by the clock,
I steal a moment from this tyrant, time,
by setting myself goals that will unlock
a minute here and there to write a rhyme.

Despite the lateness of this given hour,
I let my muse dictate, control my life;
the flowing words defy all time, empow'r
as words ink pages quickly as I write.

Alas, those stolen moments have a price,
and sleeping in 'til noon is how I pay;
but time is just a manmade clock device—
electric light extends the light of day.

I realise I cannot win with time,
it never lets me cheat or cross the line.

Chronic Insomnia

When sleep eludes, the body will not rest,
controlled by mind's insistent consciousness
to triumph over sleep with its success—
and sap the body of all stimulus.

When dawn brings light, the night has passed us by,
and tiredness has weakened energy;
no matter how we battle, how we try,
the only thing that's left is lethargy.

Then suddenly we fall into a slumber,
and nothing wakes us as our body naps;
a daytime sleep will further re-encumber
and bring the night to life, we can't relax!

This vicious circle is responsible
for making waking days impossible.

City Grime

The concrete city looms above the crowd
and dwarfs the people walking on the earth;
the busy streets now leach a fuming cloud,
as taxis buzz about for all they're worth.

A lifeless neon flicker lights the night,
as rain pours over urban life in town—
and no one stops to speak, they are in flight,
as time is of the essence, or they drown.

To slow the clock without a cost involved,
allow yourself to be a millionaire—
escape the madness, problems are dissolved—
when leaving cities for a breath of air.

The ugly game inside the city walls,
will cover skin with grime until it crawls.

Company Policy

The company was rotten at the core,
and from the top the workload was released;
the pressure was immense as it was war,
with fewer staff, compression had increased.

When at the bottom of the pile, the crush
had sucked and drained the blood out of each head;
and soon they turned into a zombie slush—
a place where you could see the walking dead.

The peanuts paid to monkeys for their time
where great demands were made of everyone,
the bullying was rife, it was a crime—
as many of the employees would run.

And I will not forget that awful job—
I likened it to working for the Mob.

Debt

The dreadful shadow hung below the light
and clung to thought like gloomy stormy rain;
there was no sun, and morning wasn't bright,
and daily life grew menacing with pain.

The mood was growing with an anxious doubt,
with no relief from what there was to come—
it seemed as though the problem had much clout
to ruin every moment, dim the sun.

The only way the doom would have release
was when the victim drank into a stupor;
the trouble melted, momentary peace,
but soon reality destroyed the future.

As debt can be a noose around the neck,
and like a sunken ship, leave just a wreck.

Deceitful Treachery

The treachery of those deceitful souls
who steal and care not how another suffers;
they leave a trail of devastating holes
when sacrificing other human brothers.

The selfish acts that take another life,
a murderous, emotional revenge;
upsets the status quo by causing strife,
resulting in much grief, as it offends.

The truth reveals the scars that never heal,
betrayal has a bitter evil taste;
and when a heart is forged with sturdy steel,
no one can break the cycle of such waste.

Eventually history records,
disloyalty will never bring rewards.

Dirty Clothes, Clean Hands

He fell on times so hard, sleep was deprived,
with little food to eat— life incomplete;
and on the filthy streets he did not thrive—
he lived close to the earth on cold concrete.

His clothes were dirty, but his hands were clean,
he never harmed another, God was near;
and humbled by the simple things in green,
bewildered by a life that wasn't clear.

From grief and anguish, to the grubby city,
survival bent his mind into this chaos;
he felt the crying shame and shunned the pity,
as life was mixed with irony and pathos.

Escaping from one struggle to another,
with changing seasons, shortened was his summer.

Disturbing Messages

I know I should have closed my eyes and slept,
but noticing a message, had to look;
and late at night my world just got upset,
a business matter had me on the hook.

I didn't sleep a wink, my mind was spinning,
with what to do, and when and how to answer;
awake all night the words I read were flitting
and stalked me like a zealous prowling panther.

I vowed to never check communication
when it's too late to activate replies;
as we don't need this adverse information—
disturbing, keeping sleep from weary eyes.

Turn all devices off and meditate—
and never check your emails when it's late.

Don't Flaunt the Rules

To flaunt the rules, defy the laws of life,
may cause a painful rift, or steal the joy
of those who have worked hard amid the strife—
behaviour such as this will soon annoy.

We learn that self-respect will have a price,
this means we cannot please ourselves alone;
but think of others, take this good advice,
communities want heroes to be known.

Obeying rules can sometimes be a pain,
but often they protect and also serve
to keep us all in line and quell the rain,
we work together, get what we deserve.

But breaking rules will end with much regret,
your path to happiness could be upset.

Elvis Lives

The ravages of time worn on her face,
the extra pounds had lingered on her middle;
her sunken eyes and frown lines have no grace
she always thought that life was just a giggle.

She struggles now, arthritis pains her knees,
but nothing stops desires to shop in town;
or pop for coffee, bagel filled with cheese—
her worn out shoes have never let her down.

Today she spots a bag she'd like to buy,
to bring a memory of youthful days;
with Elvis blazoned boldly on the side—
remembering his hips would always sway.

Inside her heart she's just a teenage girl—
the fake facade outside now hides a pearl.

Embroidered Thoughts

When peace begins to calm our troubled mind
we notice all the little things in life;
a tiny insect ploughing through the land—
a bird aloft avoiding all the strife.

We humans have the privilege to choose,
as many diverse creatures have no say;
so never waste a moment, be confused
your actions will impact the world today.

Imagine if no flowers filled our park,
our trees devoid of leaves, no butterflies;
as nature never moans about the dark,
the cloud, the storm or whether sun will rise.

Appreciate the moments you have left,
no looking back, regrets leave us bereft.

Empty Chairs

Around my table I have empty chairs—
a soulless wooden table now remains,
where hands once joined together in some prayers,
and hot drinks shared have left their burning stains.

The ghosts of yesterday are now my gifts,
my memories recall those conversations,
and in the air my Grandma's perfume drifts—
I hear the sound of raucous celebrations.

Now young new faces fill those seats of old,
we share a diff'rent time, another place—
the past I won't forget, it's forged in gold,
in grains of wood, my memories I trace.

My own chair will be empty someday too,
remembrances in passing will renew.

England is Sinking

Oh England with your stoic rhetoric,
for centuries you've spoken from the heart;
I always thought I knew what made you tick,
now bad decisions tear our world apart.

An Island left to drift without a paddle—
our friends abroad have turned their back on us;
the shortages have been an uphill battle,
we left without a word, and missed the bus.

Recovery is hard, we are not strong,
now weak and unprotected from the tide.
Opinion rules, is speculation wrong?
Are we afloat or sinking inside pride?

I'm witnessing first-hand the foolishness
we're victims of our stoic stupidness.

Ensnared by Love

The journey proved to be impossible
as not all hearts are open, some have walls;
and I was fooled, my love unstoppable,
left only with an ache, grief was the cause.

As captive was my heart, it was ensnared
with so much love to give, devotion won,
and it was well received— but never shared,
the anguish deep inside had just begun.

But over time resilience did win,
the lack of understanding would reveal
a cold and bitter soul enmeshed with sin,
where scars of long ago would never heal.

The future had a light that shone on me;
I've put this all behind me, now I'm free.

Escape to Silence

The thing I love the most in life is silence,
such peace and quiet held in high esteem;
a noisy world where there is no compliance,
is when I want to let go of a scream.

If only I could turn the volume down,
so that the silence soothes away my tear;
and when I'm on the beach or in the town,
the boats, the cars, the singers burn my ear.

But when I am alone up in the mountains,
I hear a pin drop on the solid floor;
there are no rustling trees or water fountains,
the rigid rock is silent— I restore.

The setting orb upon the wave is mute—
the sun and sea in silence I salute.

Exposing our Heart

When keeping private all of our affairs,
do we then ban a stranger from our heart;
and when including them inside our prayers,
will this mean that humanity will spark?

Our fellow men, our brothers and our sisters—
we need each other, life is full of stress
the comfort that we seek will heal our blisters,
and banish sorrow hiding in distress.

But please be cautious with your choices here,
as strangers can bring trouble to our door,
and scatter happiness that we hold dear,
with problems that we really can't ignore.

And once exposed, our privacy has gone,
how vulnerable are we to the con.

Fag Ends

The human habit leaves a bitter taste,
the debris left by smoking in the gutter;
and what about the stain that we can trace
on lungs, the blackened ash that makes us splutter.

We gag at fags, the drags of spiky crags
that scars the body with internal cancer;
and still the chimneys burn with heavy lags—
the bellowing slows down a graceful dancer.

A puff, a chuff, the stuff is rough enough
to fill the body with a warning sign;
the habit will eventually be gruff
the art of breathing will be in decline.

So heed advice to stop the smoking soon,
inhaling smoke can kill an afternoon.

Fake Facades

A perfect home, all bright and full of light,
a brand new car, all shiny on the drive;
the gardens well attended, blooms delight,
surrounded by a future set to thrive.

The fragrant rose facade with perfumed scent,
the clean and crisp appearance spelt success;
a well-built firm foundation represents—
good fortune might be blessed at this address.

Behind the doors, the story was untold,
a secret kept of horror deep within;
abusive words and actions wild and bold,
were buried deep in tempers that were thin.

Impressions can be false, there was no spark
inside this home where it is cold and dark.

Fallen Goddess

His mistress, once a Goddess, young and keen
and over time her sunken eyes lost spark;
her body ravaged by the drug routine—
so many clients left their bruising mark.

No longer is there music in her step,
her skinny frame is overdosed and done;
there are no words, as all of them inept,
as she cannot be saved from what's begun.

She has no prayers, as life has been unkind
she fell into a den she cannot leave;
without a fix then she might lose her mind,
the stupor numbs, so she can never grieve.

His mistress looks up at the stars at night,
and begs to end this life-long dreadful fight.

False Advertising

The advertisers draw the public in,
their product is for sale to everyone;
and when you buy, they're underneath your skin,
to purchase more, the sales pitch has begun.

Recruiting allies might just bend the rules,
the fight to gain some popularity;
as empty candy smiles are just for fools
who cannot see this keen dexterity.

And when something goes wrong, you can't get through
the lines are busy, no one wants to know;
you realise their advert was untrue,
and you are left with nowhere else to go.

Beware who you believe when reading news,
as many smile to cheat and to confuse.

Finding Peace

When thinking of the flowers, birds and bees,
a moment of perfection held in time;
how privileged am I, the one who sees,
recording charming beauty in a rhyme.

The colourful array of blooms outside,
a song at dawn inspiring me to wake;
the foliage alive with bees provide
a sense of compromise with give and take.

And only humans fight among themselves,
refusing to concur and understand;
division in our culture overwhelms—
there's always someone's ego in command.

In nature there is peace and harmony—
but we, the people, often disagree.

Fingers Truly Burnt

The cruel bitter warring words may spout,
when kindness has no place inside a heart
that has so much disgrace and little clout,
and so the hate will spill and tear apart.

Some never see the error of their ways
and go to graves without remorse or doubt;
and littered are the streets with all those braves,
who tried to gift their love— but were knocked out.

Is there a remedy? Is there a cure?
And if there were, would this be well received?
Forgiveness only means we still endure—
the one who has no heart and has deceived.

So many times I've heard the same excuses,
and still we're served with hatred and abuses.

Flirting with Flattery

The flattery I know to have false roots
delivered to my ears with pleasing notes;
although untruths inside my mind refutes—
attention to my ego wins some votes.

I let the praise adorn my inner soul,
to lift my spirit, bring my smile alive;
and yet I feel I'm under some control,
as on the compliments I seem to thrive.

Reality soon dawns when truth reveals,
that having one's own way comes with a price;
as puffery is empty and conceals
the reason why a stranger might entice.

Be flattered, never fooled by what you hear,
and keep a level head, with vision clear.

Flowers Mourn our Loss

A tribute standing proud among the green,
a message left of memories once bright;
these flowers indicate a life so keen,
now gone is her bright cheerfulness and light.

Her memory is in the air we breathe—
how vivid is her spirit every day;
in tasks, in scenes, in prayers we can bequeath
our thanks for her, she touched us in that way.

She'll never be forgotten, she still lives—
within the hearts of those who care and share;
the sadness that we feel, we must forgive—
for life is cruel, we are all aware . . . .

that loss can leave an emptiness inside,
and in those flowers, all of us confide.

Flying to Southern Islands

They gathered, young and old, late afternoon,
the breezy chill meant Autumn leaves would fall;
and it was time to make their fearful move,
and travel south, they heard a silent call.

And those who couldn't fly were left behind,
to face a winter in the cold and damp;
the date was set, positions now assigned,
and to the sky intrepid flocks would map.

The journey long and hard, but in their sights—
they saw their summer island, their retreat;
and one by one they landed from great heights,
triumphant and exhausted were the fleet.

They counted heads and some had lost their way
but most of them enjoyed their holiday.

A flock of birds will share the lead of the V and rotate throughout the migratory flight. Therefore, as the leaders tire, they fall further back in the flock and the birds behind will take over. This indicates that the lead would change quite often during a very long flight. How amazing is that! They have several co-pilots. Nature never fails to astound me.

Followed by Ghosts

I'm followed by the ghosts of bygone years,
as history is steeped in every stone;
the spectres walk the grounds where there were tears,
regrets that cannot heal in buried bone.

The wars, the chores the open doors and tours,
as we invite today's new eyes to see;
the buildings have remained, we pace the floors,
and soak up all the history for free.

Preserved within the walls are many ghosts,
they roam around at night, they own the town;
and keep alive the atmospheric hosts
who guard this Tudor city with their crown.

I saw the Queen this morning in her robes,
we Tudor lovers love an English rose.

For Indira

This stylish girl holds all the attributes
to be admired by family and friends;
her heart is pure and even in disputes
she has the grace to let her love extend.

Today she celebrates a special year,
as birthdays always bring such happiness;
I send my love and hope to shed a tear
of joyfulness that's instantaneous.

My wish for you is that you smile all day,
enjoy some cake and drink a glass of wine;
and soon we'll be united in a way
that always brings us pleasure every time.

I raise my glass and drink to my sweet girl,
she'll always be my perfect precious pearl.

For Tina

The candle flame has weakened over time,
the light has dimmed, it was so long ago—
your life so cruelly ended, with no climb,
as suddenly you weren't allowed to grow.

The loss was suffered by those who were close,
leukaemia had taken all control;
and powerless to help, when needed most,
no chance to compensate or make you whole.

And so the tears would fall, they wet our eye,
and devastating grief imprisoned many;
I watched and saw the congregation cry,
as everything was lost and felt so heavy.

My poem here remembers when you smiled
enlightened was the world, we were beguiled.

Foraging for Words

When reading, learning from a page of words,
our education widens from the knowledge;
and brains are overloaded with concerns,
the more we know, the more we want to forage.

We're never satisfied 'til truth is found,
our thirst increases— curiosity
becomes a big obsession, quite profound,
a journey through another's prophecy.

And sometimes hearts are scarred by those who know,
and innocence is lost, our ignorance—
replaced with wisdom as words overflow,
our eagerness becomes indifference.

To be selective when we choose a book—
might mean there are some books best overlooked.

Ghosts of Westminster Abbey

The graves entombed inside this church of old,
as history tells of a Royal tale;
the Kings and Queens, the Knights, their stories bold;
now sleepy bones no longer speak and wail . . .

or teach and preach and burn those left in tears,
the pomp and state of rulers at their worst,
thought they would live beyond their human years—
alas all buried, grounded, even cursed.

Now turned to dust just like the rest of us,
with no distinction from a pauper's grave;
as when you're dead, you might as well be dust,
when silenced by our death, no words can rave.

And only those who left behind a gift,
will be remembered, as they're surely missed.

God's Liberating Army Band

The army marched, a mission in their sights,
they're fighting for the liberty of souls;
and in their uniforms they are great knights,
who save the world, when on their keen patrols.

I hear them playing music in the street,
the melodies are hymns I used to cheer,
and when I was a girl, I'd feel the beat
to sing along to songs I loved to hear.

This faithful band of soldiers get my vote,
they always find the time for someone lost;
attention offered, gladly they devote—
no matter who you are, or what the cost.

These soldiers of the Lord are worth a mention,
their mission is to soothe, relieve the tension.

Since 1885 the Salvation Army have had a Family Tracing Service to reconcile family members who have lost contact with each other.
Onward Christian Soldiers Marching as to War. A Hymn written by Sabine Baring-Gould

Good Versus Evil

For killing's sake, one man will kill for joy,
the power and the ego warms his blood;
a trigger poised, he plans to take, destroy,
intolerance is rife, and he may judge.

Another man is born to save a life,
compassion drives his soul with charity,
with skill, becomes a surgeon with a knife—
he mends and nurtures with integrity.

Between the good and evil there is choice,
our destiny has roots in attitude;
and all of us deserve to have a voice,
we gain esteem bestowing gratitude . . .

and pray the good wins over evil deeds,
the Devil tempts and sometimes he succeeds.

Hail Macbeth

The throne it begs, Macbeth will spill some blood—
encouraged by the darkness of his mind;
confirmed by myths, decisions are misjudged
and killing has a need to be unkind.

With murderous intentions ruled by fear,
as cruelty with madness played a part;
the stench of death will never disappear
the devil has a cold unfaithful heart.

And what is done can never be undone,
the path to hell is strewn with dead remains;
the haunting truth has only just begun,
intensified by many bloody stains.

To kill for power, only to discover,
no peace exists behind deceitful cover.

Hapless Hamlet

One cold dark night a ghost begins to stalk,
appealing to his son to seek revenge;
the stench of murder lingers, it can talk
beyond the grave such treacheries transcend.

As retribution eats the soul within,
and grief and hate are cocktails set to flood;
for Hamlet wants to right this wrongful sin,
resulting in some vengeful spilling blood.

No winners in malignancy and spite
as poison has a tendency to kill,
and Hamlet had the will to start the fight,
once wronged he knew that fam'ly blood would spill.

Reprisals end in death and scar forever,
this tragedy was flawed in its endeavour.

Heads may Roll

How heavy lies the burden of great power—
the lonely place where judgements can be blurred;
and all around are threatening the tower—
as heads will roll for what has just occurred.

And those who lead with treachery will pay,
there is no place to hide when day is done;
as witnesses will note and pave the way
with sweet revenge, when guilty verdicts come.

When choosing seats of power, please beware—
that eyes are watching everywhere you look;
and if your true intention is not fair,
then hell will follow when they throw the book.

As fending foes that snap like packs of hounds,
will deafen with their mighty deadly sounds.

His Warm Embrace

I like it best when he sees me, and smiles—
he recognises how my heart has jumped;
despite our years together, and our miles,
we still have fun when meeting up for lunch.

He always looks his best, and smells divine,
and greets me with a long and loving kiss,
as passion tantalises through my spine,
secure his warm embrace— I reminisce.

But most of all I love him for his mind,
his loyalty, his empathy for others;
he taught me what it means to love mankind—
to keep the faith and always love my brothers.

Unselfishly stability he gives,
I learned a lot from him— his spirit lives.

Historic Hindsight

If I could turn the clock, change history,
adjust with hindsight misdemeanours there—
correct the deeds that taunt my memory,
and lay to rest the horrors, and repair.

Now that I know that life gave me so much,
returns that I have revelled in and gained;
the love I gave, and love received through touch,
oh how my luck in life had really changed.

Would I be free from argument within?
Would changes really help me sleep at night?
Do I believe my path would have less sin,
or are my dreams a foolish, selfish plight?

When looking back I wish I'd understood,
those anxious souls who didn't see the good.

Holding back the Tide

When worried thoughts control the day to day,
and everywhere we turn, the mind is heavy;
as stress impacts a life, and can dismay—
preventing happiness to make us merry.

With floods of problems, some may not be real,
and drowning steals our breath with suffocation;
the information stream is strong as steel—
as inner thoughts need little stimulation.

Release from problems that may not exist
takes strength to quell a tide that ebbs the flow;
deflect the negativity, resist
and focus on reality we know . . .

to fret about a problem that's imagined—
is wasted energy, when nothing's happened.

Hypocritical Faith

Those hypocrites who hide behind the cross—
profess to be a faithful loyal friend;
and when their view is tested, they then toss
opinions, accusations— condescend.

No loving words, but fire and brimstone bursts—
a crazed inhuman rant becomes the rule;
believers who are true, are not perverse—
their hearts are open, never are they cruel.

Not all converts to faith are honest men,
and some portray self-righteous traits with pride—
beware those souls who hide behind a pen
and write as though they want to be your guide.

As ravenous are wolves behind facades
that falsely guide with their cheap flawed charades.

I Learned about Love

I fell in love not knowing just how deep—
as youth allows great freedom of the heart;
a rosy path I walked, it was unique,
and I believed our bond would always chart.

I didn't see the signs that love would fail,
as all I saw was strength within my song;
the days and nights were fresh and never stale,
our love was fine, together we belonged.

Alas this love would blind me with its rule,
rejection swiftly took my breath away;
and broken was my heart, I was a fool,
abandoned and betrayed by this display.

And looking back I learned to be aware,
to study words and deeds before I share.

I Want it Now!

We want it all, today we have it now,
no waiting, and no patience will we gift;
deliver us our hearts desire somehow,
indulging in this grandeur, we insist!

We tap in our request on our computer,
and languish in our bed beyond midday;
arriving is our meal upon a scooter—
as we can have it all, if we can pay!

The culture of today has changed so much,
the world, it can be summoned to our feet;
it makes us lazy, selfishly we rush
as speed is of the essence to compete.

Fast food, and fast deliveries are winning,
there's something scary in this new beginning.

Ignite a Spark

When time is in abundance, we can dance—
in youth when we are free from ageing woes;
the endless hours devoted to romance—
so joyous, never thinking how it slows.

We live and learn and earn, and make amends,
and suffer loss, enjoy the warmth of love;
in life we suffer enemies— make friends—
we're thankful for our faith and hope above.

But in the end we say goodbye to life,
as no one lives forever, death will steal;
and in amongst the happiness and strife,
we're grateful for the chance to make it real.

Whilst there is breath within, we make our mark,
invent, ignite and light a magic spark.

Igniting War

The chronicles of war tell me a tale—
it starts with some corruption in the mind;
someone in power views a small detail
and blows it up 'til it is redefined.

A personal rebuff, historic jibe—
can fuel a fire, until the blaze is hot;
the repercussions start a deathly ride,
and soon a small detail— becomes a plot.

If only this, if only that— could change
the sequence of events that had a voice.
Conveniently, enemies are blamed,
and in the eyes of others, there's no choice . . .

retaliation shouts like it's a right
and no one doubts the reigniting spite.

Ignorance

When cluelessness becomes a prideful thing,
and those who try to fool us with their knowledge—
are ignorant, pretending to be king,
we're left with lies until we try to forage.

Stupidity may take us on a ride—
until the facts are plainly visible,
and learning truth will always be our guide,
explaining something inexplicable.

If ignorance is holding back the flow,
investigation opens up our world;
and everything will change once we can know,
to speak with expertise will be our pearl.

To understand means we can then decide,
and not be fooled by someone who has lied.

Imperfect Me

My imperfections manifest with age,
now I accept my flaws, and my mistakes,
there is no shame in scribbles on the page—
they trace despair, my bruises and my scrapes.

My learning never stops, I want to know,
and even when I stumble, and I fall,
as long as I retain my inner glow,
I can confirm, I'll never know it all.

To seek perfection means there is no peace,
the constant fight to get it right is real—
relax, enjoy, embrace that sweet release,
the best that I can give will still appeal.

To seek magnificence, will make me weak-
forgive my flaws, they make me quite unique.

Imperfections

It is our imperfections that incite
another soul to see our human trait;
connection in this moment sees a light,
and opens up a new inventive gate.

As none of us are perfect, we are flawed,
by life, by circumstances, by our greed;
we want it all, we pray our ego soars,
and think we are the best when thoughts are freed.

To get the most from life we must allow
our fellow men to shine, enjoy the scene;
a bed of roses yearns to show us how
to show appreciation, love is keen.

Be grateful that we still have much to earn,
as being perfect means we never learn.

In Silent Thought

When in my silent private thoughts of you,
recalling precious moments in the dark,
I drown my eye in wistful tears that queue
in floods of echoes left upon my heart.

Some call it grief, and some may call it joy,
as memories harass or spark some passion—
impressions of this time will not annoy,
but fill me with emotional compassion.

A legacy of love within my girls,
who had a Father with a golden gift—
to nurture with the kindness he unfurled
and in such happy times, I start to drift.

And in my waking hours on my own,
my thoughts of you mean I am not alone.

Intimidation

A threat may not reveal itself with force
manipulation has two silent feet,
it creeps inside your bones with no remorse,
as bullying can also be discreet.

Behind a mask there are some wicked tyrants
who hide their true identity from us;
but sure enough they break away from silence,
to let their tongue lash out with bloody cuts.

Oppressors soon run out of steam in time,
when failing to achieve their final goal;
and if you feel effects of such a crime,
then know you're not alone with this control.

In every walk of life there will be one
who wants to rule you with their unjust thumb.

Jack the Halloween Zombie

The skeletal remains of Jack the lad
rise up into a zombie in October;
he keeps the names of those upon a pad,
that he intends to scare when he is sober.

And those who had a hand in his demise,
he'll haunt until they beg for him to stop;
and stomachs will be full of butterflies—
the horror will ensure their jaws will drop.

As every year it's Jack who has the fun,
he smells like he has died a thousand times;
the nightmares he creates are overdone,
and those who did him wrong will pay for crimes.

He dances like he's on the set of Thriller,
and every move he makes chills like a killer.

Jake the Tabby Cat

My cat, he prowls beneath the moon and stars,
his sharpened claws are ready, just in case,
and from the tree he causes no alarms
concealed and eager is he for the chase.

His wild and focused instinct is in charge,
this tiger on the loose commands the night;
the neighbourhood is safe when he's at large,
no mouse would dare to venture, stars too bright.

But he retires at one to go to bed,
he disappears and terminates his capers.
At dawn when he is happy to be fed—
his roving eye will check for new invaders.

My pussycat is gentle and he's sweet,
although I know he's fearless in the street.

Journey Home

My feet sink in resilient blades of grass,
I feel the cold damp earth seep through my bones
sensations penetrate inside, harass—
my heart, it skips in humble, thankful tones.

I found a place on earth to soothe my soul—
in England's green and fervent pleasant lands;
nowhere I'd rather be than here, my home,
a place where I am understood by clans.

With roots in history I'm born to riches,

where Kings and Queens have walked and sat on thrones,
abundant wealth within the towns and cities,
in England where the banter here atones.

My ashes will be scattered in the park,
forever I will listen to the lark.

Justice for the People

When justice speaks and falls on deafened ears,
and scatters every faithful heart for miles;
the questions that arise are full of fears,
as tyranny intrudes with shifty smiles.

The evidence is lost, and prejudice—
is foremost in the minds of those who boast;
as lies are bigoted, incredulous,
and truth is hidden, pales into a ghost.

The Bible says the weak, the destitute—
deserve the same respect as those in power;
oppression is the devil's institute,
and justice will prevail, and even flower.

And even the afflicted earn the right,
to just and fair behaviour without spite.

Kindness costs Nothing

The merciful retain the grace of God,
those kindly souls who never can be tempted;
unmoved are they to use an iron rod
or on a spiteful path are they directed.

For those who keep the summer in their hearts,
their optimism casts a comfort blanket;
no riches are required to set apart
a spirit that can offer such a banquet.

As kindness, a commodity so short,
exists in very few we come across;
but when we find this helpful warm support,
it thaws with its potential to defrost.

We have the pow'r to change another's luck,
and all it takes is courage and some pluck.

Kindness Viewed Within

The kindness that a blinded eye can see,
a sense of warmth fixated on the good;
without the prejudice of viewing me,
the beauty from within is understood.

And in the darkness, light begins to shine,
as deep connections birth within the heart;
a touch that speaks a thousand words is mine,
creating grief whenever we're apart.

Our senses never fail us in the dark,
we recognise the hostile, hear the sound;
and we are drawn to those who have a heart,
the beat is loud and always is profound.

The empathy of one who cares, despite
the loss of viewing us with perfect sight.

Knife Angel

The Angel pleads to end a life of crime
where blades have cut and injured human flesh;
if only we could change things in our time,
reset a mind-set, nurture and refresh.

Forgive our fellow men, insight good will,
bring love instead of hate to everyone;
re-educate the young, give them a skill—
to understand each other— overcome.

In each event, two victims pay the cost,
the perpetrator ends his life of freedom;
the injured suffers pain, or life is lost,
and neither finds a place to call their Eden.

Intriguing is this statue made of knives—
to stimulate morality— it thrives.

This unique statue has toured the England and it is at present in Lichfield.
It is a stature made entirely of knives in the shape of an angel with hands
outstretched, pleading for mercy in an effort to appeal to those who carry
knives with the intent to cause harm, to stop this heinous crime. It has a
striking appearance.

Last Goodbyes

Although we parted as good friends that day,
a sense of sweet relief ran through my veins;
goodbyes are never easy, so they say—
resigned was I to let go of my chains.

I saw you standing there and still remember,
that sad bewildered look you gave to me;
and left was I alone in sweet surrender—
decisions made by you would always be.

Reflecting on events are now long gone
I knew I'd never see you here again;
no more would I be broken, time moved on,
though memories are leaking from my pen.

Your swift departure left a trail of pain,
and nothing can remove that heartless stain.

Learning from History

When listening to children speak their truth,
it's raw and honest, it will touch your heart
and sometimes they will tell you they dispute
a rule they do not think is very smart.

I argue, but remind myself that they're young,
with no experience of life outside;
how vulnerable are they with their tongue,
but have developed ego in their pride.

I point them in directions where they think
and then decide to test their theories;
I'm never disappointed when I wink,
they have the answers to their own queries.

We learn to work with problems once we know,
that history will help us all to grow

Leave Behind a Rhyme

We never know how long we've got to live,
and life is never easy on our own . . .
but every time we let go, and we give—
another seed of love we've surely sown.

To leave behind some kindness in our wake,
a message filled with tenderness and love,
ensures that other hearts will never break . . .
and memories forever shine above.

We have one chance to leave behind some thoughts,
to keep humanity alive and keen . . .
before the final curtain falls, transports
us to our resting place, where we're not seen.

Our life is short so make the most of time,
and leave behind a mystery in rhyme.

Left Alone

Since I was left alone I took the reins,
and never did I let go of my goal;
with great determination— cut my chains,
allowed myself to take complete control.

No longer do I pander to your whims,
or listen to your early morning moans,
I've stepped into a new life, it begins
with how a self-indulgent life atones.

Was I a fool to take care of your needs,
when mine were just ignored and overlooked?
My heart is happy, it no longer bleeds,
and on this new found freedom I am hooked.

Who'd ever thought that living by myself
would be this opulent— and good for health.

Let Sorrow Go

How can a grief-filled heart find happiness?
When day's oppressive gloom's not eased by night,
and when the day and night undo all rest,
where can we find the courage for the fight?

And tortured is the soul, the spirit fails
to see the sun, the stars, the moon, the earth;
the flowers and the trees renew their sails,
but Spring has no reward, despite new birth.

Our sorrow isolates our observations,
if only we could open up our eyes—
and see that life is full of compensations,
to quell the misery, create the highs.

To see a brand new world, a chance to live,
and find love in your heart, yourself forgive.

Lichfield Market

The thriving throbbing trading stalls are open,
attracting crowds to market square in town;
from fruit to soap, the choices are a token—
to diverse shopping licensed by the crown.

As long ago King Stephen granted rights,
to traders who can sell their wares for cash;
and since that date the market here delights
and often bargains sell within a flash.

I hear the trader on the fruit stall shout,
his accent is as rough as rough can be;
his dedication to the sell, devout,
as long as you're prepared to pay the fee.

My favourite stall sells homemade fairy cakes,
you cannot beat those buttery fresh bakes.

Life is Rich

How rich this life I live as I don't want,
as all I need is here in such abundance;
and lucky me, I am so nonchalant,
and glide through life, and never feel redundant.

There is so much to do, I pray that time
does not desert me in my hour of need;
how rich is life when young, it seems a crime
to age with such a racing rapid speed.

I realise that what I want is time,
the greed inside will not allow me rest;
and cheated am I by the clock, a sign—
that only those with youth can beat their chest.

But I will find contentment in my past,
as memories of mine were built to last.

Lily Pond

Beneath the murky pond there lurks a root,
a thread of life that's delicately woven;
it reaches to the light, there is a shoot,
that eagerly with petals starts to open.

And like a tray of coloured iced delights—
amid the canker, pure white virgin blooms;
are floating on the surface that ignites
a passionate response to their costumes.

As here I witness ostentatious gifts,
a garden on the waters of a pond;
these flowers lift their faces in the drifts,
and swim within a stagnant putrid pong.

This miracle is found among the rot,
a pure white lily finds a sunny spot.

Listen and Learn

The greatest gift to give someone is time,
our undivided therapy, to listen;
to hear another person's plight, their rhyme—
a point of view, their soulful heartfelt mission.

Affording someone time to tell their story,
to read their verse, absorbing what they say;
supporting and rewarding this with glory,
as everyone has tales that save the day.

So go ahead and read and hear those words,
we learn more by allowing details in;
and sharing thoughts, just like our tweeting birds,
will spread our wings, we'll fly above the din.

To open up your heart to other news,
unites the people, spreads our diff'rent views

Love can Disappoint

When bad behaviour has no consequences
then it proceeds with no impediment;
and nothing stops the damage of offences
when punishments are lame and indolent.

Allowing someone access to your heart
when there is some mistrust and doubtful thought;
we aid, abet, encourage love to start,
believing that we won't become distraught.

Our intuition warns us in advance,
take note and heed the signs before a fall;
and when a romance sours there is a chance,
that hurtful words and deeds will not be small.

Be strong and honest, keep your self-respect,
not everyone gives love as we expect.

Love can Hurt

A loyal love that stood the test of time,
a faithful, warm, enduring, kind connection;
and nothing broke the bond, this love was fine—
serene and peaceful moments in reflection.

United in their thoughts, no words of doubt,
and passion would ignite their hearts with fire;
together they were steadfast and devout,
and happiness would reign and never tire.

But nothing lasts forever, so they say—
and tragedy befell these star crossed lovers;
an accident took one of them away,
the other left to mourn in grief, and suffers.

We never know how cruel life can be—
when opening our heart, we are not free.

Love Fades

A love that will not shake at its foundation,
an everlasting union of two minds;
until one dies there is no separation;
a love like this is full of happy times.

And by a tempest, love will never quake,
the strength within is indestructible;
and compromise means there is give and take
a balance that is incorruptible.

But nothing lasts forever, time is harsh,
eroding with a rust that rots the root;
a fading memory of threads now sparse
that crumble at the touch— there is no fruit.

And over time there is a diff'rent view,
as boredom can destroy what once was new.

Mentors

Our mentors give us hope, they let us shine,
encouraging our inner thoughts to grow;
and soon we fly, inspired by design--
as all that we have learned-- begins to flow.

Our pen is touched by magic, inks the page
our words selected from a bed of roses;
describing scenes we feed the world, engage--
a story packs a punch, as it discloses.

And giving thanks to those who took the time
to teach us with great expertise and skill--
the mentor can sit back and feel sublime,
we prodigies can write and we can thrill.

Agreeing to lay bare our heart and soul
we harness artistry and reach our goal.

Mob Culture

Can crowds persuade? Manipulate the law?
Can public anger hang a guiltless man?
Reprisals of such fear make us withdraw—
allow injustice— favouring the clan.

Without the facts we judge and persecute,
condemn and sentence others to a crime;
beware misinformation in dispute—
as lies will stain our history in time.

No matter who we are we're vulnerable
to mobs of men who cry for our demise;
the consequences are insufferable,
so keep your counsel truthful, let it rise.

If you shipwreck your conscience in a mob
adrift, you'll drown— of honesty be robbed.

Money

The face of money, measured, priced and weighed—
can be the catalyst for theft and murder;
as greed and power cast a deadly shade,
and money is the single keen observer.

The bargaining with hearts and stolen kisses,
the sacrifices made to gain a dime—
will shock the world when some require such riches
to live a life where money is sublime.

Contentedness is absent, there's no joy,
as pleasure's not the object of desire;
the focus on the stockpile will annoy—
and discontent will frequently transpire.

The root of evil has a dismal face;
and money can be blamed for this disgrace.

My Lovely Valentine

My Valentine has given all his time—
bestowing all affection and attention;
I'm blessed with roses, everyone is mine,
they show me love was always his intention.

And I return with gifts straight from my heart,
with written words to touch his soul inside;
our years together magical and marked—
with happy times recorded and inscribed.

My Valentine has left a legacy,
another generation has his eyes;
he lives within their personality,
so many faces capture sunny skies.

My Valentine lives on into the future,
in little faces kept on my computer.

My Name

When growing up I learned to hate my name,
as hearing it meant I was in big trouble;
accused of many deeds that would inflame,
and hearing my name was an awful struggle.

At school the disrespect was evident,
the teachers called us girls by our last name;
a cold, a callous, calling of contempt,
which made my name abhorrent and inane.

But then I met the man who changed all that,
my name became synonymous with love;
he spoke my name so tenderly, in fact,
it sounded like a cooing, loving dove.

From that day forth my name has sounded kind,
the trauma of my name was in my mind.

Naive Love

How can love blind me with reality?
and fool me with its tantalising sin,
I fall into a pit, I am not free,
as love has shackled me beneath my skin.

A slave to love, surrendered to desire,
obeying every whim, I am in chains;
and breaking free would mean I would retire
from all the love I feel inside these flames.

The passion soon subsides when dawn brings truth,
unequal are the scales, my eye's impaired;
a choice has to be made, although my youth
still yearns for all the joy that has been shared.

I see the light before it is too late,
and leave before this love turns into hate.

Never Grow Old

Do we let age define us when we're old?
When gait and wrinkles mark our outer shell.
Can we retain a strand of youthful gold,
when vibrant spring infused in every cell?

An active mind controls our attitude,
encouraged by an interest in life;
and when we fail to have some gratitude,
we fall into the pit of hell and strife.

Appreciating time we spend on earth,
requires selective thinking when we age;
to concentrate on negatives can birth
a mind that will not liberate— engage.

We share a time and place with those around—
and have the right to speak and be profound.

Night Creepers

The early hours when everyone's asleep,
and silence soothes the soul as we're at rest;
the creatures of the dark will take a peep—
and creep about with freedom to infest.

The cockroaches that roam about at night,
they know our eyes are closed, they take a chance
and hide away from capture in the light—
survival is their goal when they advance.

Then suddenly electric light reveals,
disturbed are we by what is lurking there;
and under foot this little creature squeals—
diseases he will never get to share.

Beneath the cloak of darkness, insects crawl,
and when we are asleep they come to call.

Noisy Builders

They laid the deep foundations for the build,
by thumping into soil with fork lift trucks—
and concrete poured into the trenches filled,
the footings for some homes that are deluxe.

And soon the staggered bricks began to rise,
fluorescent hats and jackets bob about;
and rubber tracks delivering supplies
are beeping back and forth as workmen shout.

The noise begins at seven and the birds
are drowned out by machines that let off steam.
I never have the peace that I deserve—
as sounds of engines moaning is extreme.

To silence them would be my biggest wish,
a time when peace prevailed, I reminisce.

Offended by Words

Be not offended by the words of others,
keep precious gems within, to soothe your soul,
as no one knows the story of those brothers
their suffering, their joys, their private goals.

If strangers make assumptions, let them speak,
as you will know the truth inside your heart,
their argument is wrong and it is weak,
your honesty, integrity will chart.

As no one has the right to judge you here,
and swords that cross can start a filthy war;
keep pure your inner thoughts as you appear
uncaring of a thoughtless word— ignore.

A word in your direction was not meant
to hurt you by a stranger with intent.

Oppression Kills our Innocence

When words have lost their power in the feud,
our actions speak for us and make our point;
as empty threats will never change the mood,
and deeds will verbalise and disappoint.

We leave a trail of sorrow in our wake,
decisions we take lightly cost us dear;
but time can steer our course with give and take,
when standing up, we take control of fear.

And over time respect has to be earned,
especially when someone steals your heart;
it's hard to be that strong where love's concerned,
as grief destroys our self-esteem apart.

The fight to take control can spill some blood,
oppression kills our innocence for good.

Optimistic Song

How can a grief-filled heart find happiness?
When day's oppressive gloom's not eased by night,
and when the sorrow swears possessiveness,
how can the victim ever see the light?

And time heals only those who view with hope,
as when the heart is broken, all is lost;
we find our spirit tethered by a rope,
and willing hearts are keen to pay the cost.

We cling to memories, and bring to life,
a world where love was strong with good support,
and when we lose a husband or a wife,
foundations rock, stability distorts.

We hold onto an optimistic song,
rewinding happiness is never wrong.

Over Indulgence Kills

So many souls defeated by the clock—
they promised change, but left it far too late;
their life-style habits pinned them, like a rock—
remaining loyal to their heavy weight.

And one by one they fell to death's demise,
and ate themselves into an early grave;
obesity is always on the rise—
indulgences in too much food they crave.

The warning signs were there, they had a choice,
ignoring all their symptoms, sank the boat;
unhealthy choices hushed their final voice,
they drowned in fat, it was a heavy coat.

Do not be ill-advised— beware of food
an enemy when too much is consumed.

Packington Pig Farm

I won't forget the day I lost my sister,
her company I miss, she was my mate;
but pigs will disappear in just a whisper
I know not where they go, or what their fate.

Our life is peaceful albeit too short—
there are some rumours of a slaughter house;
I don't let all the others spoil my sport,
I love to mooch about and chase a mouse.

Then came a time when I would journey too,
complaining was a useless energy—
I didn't travel far before I knew . . .
for being pork, I paid the penalty.

Perhaps one day when pork is not so prized
the use of pigs for food will be revised.

Playa del Camison

The burning golden sand where sun beats hard
on oily limbs that bake in midday heat;
and leafy palms protect those who are charred—
those topless beauties with their bodies neat.

I sit and sip my sangria on ice,
and listen to a twelve string Spanish tune;
whilst rippling waves begin to call, entice—
and cool my hot and steamy afternoon.

Cocooned among the island folk I know—
the skies are clear, and heat begins to rise,
and British faces red and raw, now glow—
will suffer for the excess, no surprise!

Today is hot and I will keep my cool,
as keeping under cover is the rule.

Precious Nature Scenes

With nature's paint I colour every garden
if only I had power to renew;
my role is to admire the season's tartan,
and with my art preserve the magic view.

I realise each moment never lasts,
and to my memory each scene is sewn;
as nature richly oozes with contrasts,
and Winter can chill trees through to the bone.

And when the snow has covered every bloom
and stifled life with bitter icy cold;
my senses take me back to sweet perfume,
those petalled roses delicately bold.

My picture perfect scene is on my wall,
with nature's painted fantasy, recall.

Pretence

The air is filled with false desires and lies,
as no one has the stomach for the truth;
behind the scenes the congregation hides—
as secrets scandalous will not dilute.

And under carpets, swept is all the dirt,
not seen by public eyes, facades are clean;
in pretty hats and dresses, ladies flirt,
no mention of disturbing things unseen.

And only those within the inner circle
are privy to the facts that lie beneath;
the true intentions written in a journal
will never see the light or ever breathe.

Pretence can be achieved when fear is real,
ensuring that a secret is concealed.

Public Manipulation

Don't ask me to believe in lies I'm told,
when it is clear the truth is plain to see;
displays can be deceitful, also bold,
they're targeted at many just like me.

The subtleties of sweet manipulation,
have questioned everybody's true beliefs,
and changed their view with moral subjugation,
with ease, the guilty conscience suffers grief.

Strategic law behind the treachery,
is visible when looking at the truth;
it hides behind our age old memory,
indoctrinates the innocence of youth.

Beware the speaker's secretive agenda,
disguised, he is a serial offender.

Pursue your Dreams

Do not forsake your dreams, they may come true,
when inspiration rises to a peak;
your faith and hope will lead the way for you,
a cherished dream is personal, unique.

Ambitions can be real if we accept—
achieving goals takes courage and belief;
and giving up will leave us all inept,
our self-esteem is stolen like a thief.

A caterpillar had a dream one day,
his ugly coat turned into petalled wings;
he floated like a butterfly away—
a fantasy is how a dream begins.

Pursue your dreams with energy and vigour,
allow yourself to dream for something bigger.

PUTin Them UNder

(Vlad and Kim)

It is a marriage likely made in hell,
the leaders of the packs of wolves will meet;
and in a secret room they kiss and tell
of plans to kill and maim to gain the seat.

And at that table, horror will ensue,
as terrorists with bombs and hate debate;
the tyrants will then target and subdue,
to grab the land by killing to dictate.

And what about the people on the land?
Their loyalty will never be regained;
remembering, will always understand,
the suffering and murder they sustained.

The minds of men who never saw the light,
were born to leave behind historic blight.

Kim Jong Un takes an armoured train to meet Vladimir Putin for talks and offer his support to Russia in the fight to win over the control of Ukraine. This war has already cost the lives of over 47,000 Russian troops. The Mothers grieve for their sons and have no power to remove Putin from his seat.

Rainbow of Love

The flush of youth, how rosy **red** those cheeks—
a blushing bride anticipates her future;
and **orange** brings prosperity for keeps,
with energy and optimistic humour.

In Spring the **yellow** blooms deliver cheer—
as vibrant **green** depicts a fertile field;
expanding family will soon appear,
and skies are always **blue** when love is sealed.

And wisdom, intuition earned with age
as **indigo**, a colour deeply potent,
where meditation— faithful love can stage,
initiative and planning can be focused.

And finally a **violet** of passion,
humility and innocence in fashion.

Read Between the Lines

I read between the lines to understand,
the message has so much to say within,
a subtle hint can touch, it can expand
with insights to the heart, it will begin.

Behind a word, there are so many more,
the meaning hides the truth, we need to look;
as depths reveal the soul, the very core—
we find that some are just an open book.

Beware, as what you find may be surprising,
not everyone has love inside their heart;
a swinging brick might cause a big uprising,
and what you thought was love is spiteful art.

The words, just like a painting hide a secret,
and in between the lines the words reveal it.

Reading Books

I steal myself away to read my book,
and in the pages lose myself in words;
the story grabs me, I am on the hook—
inside another world, I've joined the nerds.

I'm thrown into the exploits of the writer
his mind manipulates, controls my thoughts;
I find myself on horseback as a fighter—
created scenes have visual retorts.

I have escaped into this fantasy,
with every word I'm guided through the tale,
and when I'm faced with false insanity—
I intervene, my instinct will not fail . . .

we either love the story we are told,
alternatively fables leave us cold.

Reflections Still Aflame

The morning sun reflects with golden hues,
upon the rugged mountain rough terrain;
and like the pyramid of pharaohs tomb—
this eerie, ghostly, ancient rock of Spain . . .

has witnessed many changes over years,
the joys and sorrows facing man in time;
inhabitants who left their souvenirs,
when toiling through the rock, to redesign.

We've tunnelled under mountains like a mole,
and carved our way through solid molten rock;
disturbing bygone prehistoric bone—
where secrets held beneath are under lock.

But mountains cannot move, they still reclaim—
reflections of the past are still aflame.

Man has toiled on this Canarian Island and carved tunnels through the rocks to make roads, but the mountains can never be moved, and the reflections I see today have been the same for twenty million years. A sobering thought.

Reformed Believers

The patronising minds who dig the dirt,
and tell a tale of righteousness and faith;
but deep within their mind they have been hurt,
reforming is the way they can placate.

From love to hate, the journey is historic,
and frowned upon are those with empathy;
this condescending nature is euphoric—
to elevate oneself, the remedy.

Please spare a thought for those less fortunate,
show mercy to another soul in need;
there is no black and white, don't be corrupt,
no one is perfect, let your conscience lead.

Alleviate the suffering of those
who fall into the trap that you oppose.

Returning Home

Fatigued and worn, but spirits never broken,
arriving home, the battle left some scars;
on English soil where few words could be spoken,
the bombs left buildings everywhere in shards.

A battle raged, civilians faced with terror,
the blitz left rubble in the London street;
survivors busy— ending war a pleasure,
relief that no more bombings would repeat.

And England's hero, Nelson is still standing,
a symbol of the people's strength and grit.
Trafalgar Square, a welcome sight, demanding
that life goes on, we must get on with it.

No time to mourn, there is so much to do,
although the shock of sorrow will subdue.

This poem was inspired by Jim Bartlett (Author and Poet). His popular novel called (Gavin and the Ritter von Grunholz) refers to a particular chapter in (London 1945), Gavin travels from the Dockland to RAF Biggin Hill and witnesses for the first time the devastating bombing in his homeland and how the civilians had suffered the effects of war.

To go to war and return home to chaos and mayhem after the bombings in London, must have been soul destroying, yet Gavin in this story remains optimistic about returning to his old position in the Airforce. Old habits die hard.

Revitalise your Views

When flippant words dismiss another's grief
and hide behind indifference and doubt;
they lose their chance to own some self-belief,
integrity is lost, there is a drought.

Humanity and empathy are gifts,
and those who toss them, throw away their pride,
aggressive anger deep inside persists—
the crowd have little faith, when words are tied.

An understanding word can please the ear,
can lift the light, and bring a sunny day;
and quell the showers, dry a falling tear,
just like a smile, a word can guide our way.

Be careful when critiquing, show your worth,
your kindness can revitalise, unearth.

Reviving Shakespeare's Sonnets

From one Elizabethan to another,
reviving sonnets in the present day;
as I have now become a Shakespeare lover,
inspired am I by every sunshine ray.

Although we're worlds apart, we join in song,
the melody within is loud and clear;
each word is floating off my dulcet tongue,
you might be turning in your grave my dear.

The sonnet form is famous, thanks to you,
a privilege to read them out aloud;
and nowadays they're read by very few,
so many other things amuse the crowd.

But lively are those poems in my head,
your words are still alive, although you're dead.

Ruby Tuesday

I'd never know when she'd accept the light,
as she was never chained by rhyme or reason,
and in the brightest sun or darkest night—
she would come and go with each new season.

No time to lose as life is short she'd say,
so follow dreams before it is too late;
we're dying all the time, live for today,
the past is gone, tomorrow's just a date.

So goodbye Ruby Tuesday, go and play,
I'm gonna miss you baby, come back soon;
and when you change with every single day—
remember that we shared this afternoon.

Your carefree thinking follows you around,
your heart is free and love is what you've found.

This is a sonnet about the song called (Ruby Tuesday) written by Mick Jagger and Keith Richards and performed by Melonie.

Ruth

Her jealous eye watched carefully that night,
a witness to deceit, her blood would boil;
her lover with another in her sight,
would pay a deadly price for spiteful spoil.

The pistol at her side was fully loaded,
and from the shadows she emerged with pride,
a bullet to the heart released— exploded,
he fell into the gutter, and he died.

She also paid the price for this affair,
in Holloway, the gallows, where she fell
will always be remembered and impaired
by whispers of injustice in this hell.

No woman swung for murder, laws were changed,
this was too late for Ruth, her death enraged.

*Ruth Ellis met David Blakely, a racing car driver, and they had an affair.
He betrayed her and she took revenge by shooting him dead outside The
Magdala Public House in Hampstead, London. She was found guilty of
murder and sentenced to death at Holloway prison on 13 July 1955. She was
the last woman to hang in Britain. Thousands of people protested and
signed petitions, but the sentence was carried out. Although she admitted
shooting Blakely, her mind was unstable at the time and she would have
received a much lighter sentence in today's courts.*

The last hangings took place in 1964 and it was abolished in 1969.

Saturday Distractions

The plebs are here and there, and fill the square,
where markets cram their wares into the stalls;
the hum of voices, singers, everywhere—
above the din the church bells make their calls.

I dodge between the crowd, and duck collision,
and run my errands on my weekend splurge;
must exit fast, avoid my indecision—
in case I'm swallowed whole, and don't emerge!

On Saturday when Lichfield entertains,
a city full of vibrant acrobats;
as bible pushers preach with their campaigns,
and costume lovers wear elab'rate hats!

I breathe a sigh, arriving home again,
I never want to leave my cosy den.

Shadows Captured

Those shadows tall are steeped in memories,
a trip to Dorset on a sunny day,
the family enjoying reveries—
togetherness, ensuring seconds stay.

Those stepping stones in life when times renew,
become inscribed impressions lost in time;
as fleeting as a shadow here on cue—
and sweet and warm as mulled and spicy wine . . .

and captured is the moment set on stone
to never be repeated or resumed,
and from this moment forward, overgrown—
as history will fade so very soon.

This spooky shadow inks upon the pavement—
a lifelong echo locked in entertainment.

Shadows of Life

A shadow, crystal clear as Spring stirs light,
as youthful silhouettes are sharply keen;
an energetic step is full of life—
the images on pavements clearly seen.

As Summer sun so low where statues tall
are playful shadows in romantic art,
a couple holding hands in love they Fall,
a powerful reflection of the heart.

And in the fall the shadows start to fade,
as leaves obscure the surface once so plain,
a figure standing lonely in the shade—
as pathways stain with spots of Autumn rain.

In Winter all the shadows have been cast
as memories record them in the past.

Signs of Sincerity

How sad it is to have no moral fibre,
to care not whether someone lives or dies;
no mercy shown for every last survivor,
the fellowship that gains the winning prize.

Too many hate without a rhyme or reason,
from jealousy or greed, a shadow forms;
as ice can chill just like the winter season,
and rain will fall from mighty heavy storms.

So bring a little sunshine to your day,
as smiles can brighten someone else's life;
a caring word will go a long, long way—
to quell another person's inner strife.

Sincerity begins to glow and shine,
a sign compassion is not deaf and blind.

Snubbed

Across the room their eyes had made a bond
and no one else would know their deep affection;
attraction had the power to respond
with physical and intimate direction.

Forbidden love can cross the social fringe,
but has no future in the light of day;
the thirsty urge is no more than a binge
as she would be the victim— easy prey.

Alas, when born the wrong side of the sheets,
no status means no right to pick and choose,
and soon this lass would be back on the streets,
an outcast has no right to wear the shoes.

The cold and heartless ranking is intense,
disdain will be the only recompense.

Sonnet 18 with a Difference

Shall I compare thee to an ugly toad?
Thou art grotesque and absent is all grace;
as winds shake trees and litter every road,
the winter settles on your wizened face.

Some chill just like the Devil, with their hell,
as age has given ugliness some wings;
repugnancy will never spin a spell,
or tempt a pretty flower into spring.

But thy eternal winter can still rage,
and damage special moments with your will;
remembering the tantrums on the stage,
a frightful look from you would almost kill.

So long as men can breathe, or eyes can see,
your ugly face still lives, gives life to thee.

Sonnet for Jan

I close my eyes and say a prayer for Jan
and I will miss her presence, words she wrote;
of her sweet poetry, I was a fan—
my empathy for family— devote.

And may she rest in peace and be remembered,
as many friends will pay a tribute here,
for all the fine warm poems she assembled,
and I will not forget how sweet her cheer.

I write a sonnet for my dearest friend,
how sad I feel that she has left too soon,
our grief and sorrow has no way to end,
to saddened thoughts we cannot be immune.

And I remember Jan, her kindness shone,
how sorry am I that she has now gone.

Jan was a member on a poetry site called Fanstory and she sadly died prematurely in 2023.

Soulful Sonnets

When passion fills our hearts with much desire
our ink will scroll the words we feel inside;
and suddenly expressed are vows of fire,
the rhymes that bring us joy will be our guide.

Imagination has the pow'r to give—
and every time we write, we spread a pledge;
to reconnect with others and forgive,
emotions touch, and tears will often dredge.

We laugh and cry, we moan and praise ourselves,
we dwell on things that hurt and spill our blood;
and also love, our heartfelt pride rebels,
to reach the stars and moon— desire is good.

We battle and we take charge of our days
and words will help us cope with every phase.

Spiritual Connections

Our spirit can be moved, it's versatile,
by worthy deeds with positivity—
that lift us, make us go that extra mile,
to give us inner strength, stability.

Our passion's motivated by emotion,
a spark inside will push toward success;
and with determination and devotion,
we dash toward our goal without distress.

We're spirited by life's sweet potency,
there is so much to see, so much to know;
and with polite and skilled diplomacy,
we share our love, and let it overflow.

Our human quest for company is real—
our spirit has a unique warm appeal.

Stalin's Russia

The suffering continued: it was known—
but no one knew how many starved to death;
as some lived on the flesh from human bone,
to save themselves from final chilling breath.

The dying bones of famine on the land,
the skeletal remains that shadowed youth,
they faded, could no longer walk or stand,
when hunger stole their lives, their honest truth.

The facts reported, but were never heard,
and no one could believe a word of it;
the lightweight whisper of one lonely bird—
that communism caused this to exist.

The ghosts of those who died at Stalin's hand
are rising in Ukraine to fight for land.

Holodomor, was a man-made famine that occurred in the Soviet republic of Ukraine from 1932 to 1933, it peaked in the spring of 1933. It caused a mass starvation in the grain-growing regions of Russia. Stalin tried to hide the famine and cover up the numbers of deaths in this murderous act, as millions had died and the truth was eventually reported.

Stand up and be Counted

No matter who you trust to give advice,
no one can be precise consistently;
as everyone is flawed, and not concise,
and sometimes they don't have a remedy.

The element of chance can sway the odds,
as outside influence can change results;
so keep an open mind here, just because—
a change in circumstances interrupts.

So if a hard decision can't be made,
we listen to advice, we are polite;
and never let go of our own crusade,
for what we know is truly something right.

Have courage to stand-up against the crowd,
ensuring that your word is loud and proud.

Stay Positive

Let summer leave some sunshine in your heart
and never let the winter freeze its core;
as seasons change, we can be torn apart
by heavy snow that blocks the open door.

Allow your spirit freedom, give it wings,
we have the strength within to ride the storm;
maintain an inner calm when trouble brings
a troubled path of grief, a saddened mourn.

Another day can change the status quo,
the glinting sun begins to thaw the ice,
and with it comes relief, albeit slow—
we heal ourselves with positive advice.

We have the choice to view the scene with eyes
to always see the good things, this is wise.

Sweet Embraces

How gentle is your touch, your sweet embrace,
with tender words I hear the sound of love;
the music plays and there's a kind of grace,
an atmospheric aura from above.

Surrounded am I by those perfumed roses,
my valentine has sent, to make me smile;
in every deed his loyalty exposes,
and I can feel the magic of his style.

And soon I'll hear a knock upon my door,
excitement feels me with anticipation;
and there he stands, the one that I adore,
fulfilling all my dreams and expectation.

Alas, my love, I cannot play today,
I missed my flight, there could be some delay.

Tactless Taunts

A tactless deed can root beneath the soil,
and like a weed, it strangles pretty blooms;
without attention seeds begin to spoil—
when roses die, the callousness consumes.

Just like the flu a word can spread disease,
its wings move like an eagle on the hunt;
and news will circulate upon the breeze,
as everyone will know who took the brunt.

When in disgrace, dishonour leaves a sting,
as shame can torture with its condemnation;
a scandal makes the critics wail and sing,
and months will pass before the restoration.

And those who are supportive and discreet,
allow a rogue to ambush and mistreat.

Takers and Givers

There are those souls who give their all to others.
Doctors and the nurses, we hold dear;
our mothers, fathers, sisters and our brothers
all of whom we praise and give a cheer.

And even strangers lend a helping hand.
The world is full of kindly caring people.
Beware there are another hard-luck band
who take, when praying at the local steeple.

The takers rob and steal and even kill,
disturb our life with traits they leave in blood;
and do it all to gain a little thrill,
impress their mates with evil seeds they bud.

Communities need those who contribute
so never let a good review be mute.

Tales of Life

This time, when changes take place every day,
and nothing stays the same, no anchor here;
I try to hold this moment, hope you stay,
but fate has played its hand, there is no steer.

My influence has little mastery,
the days slip by, I cannot stop the clock;
events ingrained within my memory—
like ghostly silhouettes that laugh and mock.

I realise that time has left its mark,
and I can't choose to swim against the tide;
or let emotions sadden in the dark—
tomorrow life will challenge me to ride.

And I will board the train into the future,
and write my tale of life on my computer.

Teenage Frustrations

The flippant words attack with venom's bite,
the menacing of someone who is young;
they realise that life is not quite right—
when bitterness releases from their tongue.

To kick the hornets' nest and stir the pot—
unhappiness is evident and rife;
and when solutions never hit the spot
they learn that trouble manifests in life.

And soon the penny drops— they learn to cope,
the teenage years are full of fear and dread—
but luckily support gives them some hope
to manage deep emotions in their head.

The strop, although dismissive, is a must
as teenagers think everything's unjust.

Terns try a Takeover

The terns take charge, the local pool is crowded—
with booted, suited uniforms of white;
incessantly their rule is often shrouded
by spiteful pecks that nip the hens at night.

Aggressively they push and shove the ducks,
the flock, like bullies, organise from skies;
insisting that they own the crows and rooks,
and from above are verbal with their cries.

Beware the geese are flying overhead,
they wear the jackboots, terns know who is boss;
the geese take charge of everything instead,
now these long necks are calling all the shots!

There is no doubt that geese police the pool,
and ducks and terns obey Gestapo rule.

The Burial

They gathered all black-suited in their grief,
for one who now lay cold and drained of life;
and tears were shed by mourners with belief
that painful sorrow passes in the night.

For some the torment lingers, death is quick,
the sharpness of finality brings shock;
the silent emptiness is dense and thick—
and heavily it drags and slows the clock.

Although the loss leaves dregs of memory,
our tears dry with a hopeful smiling child;
the future in our arms is bright and free—
bewilderment leaves relatives beguiled.

We pin our hopes and future on new life,
the legacy we leave behind is bright.

The Haunting of Lady Macbeth

Her bloody hands were stained, could not be cleaned,
her evil deed destroyed and left a scar;
the past could not be changed her soul redeemed,
and nightmares dogged internally with tar.

She dipped into the unknown world of murder—
now tainted was her heart, it would not mend,
and death now haunts this keen and mean observer,
no longer on her conscience can depend.

Outstanding is a debt that must be paid,
once entering the maze, there's no way out;
inside the shadows, ghosts are unafraid
appearing everywhere, with scorn they shout.

The fear brings every memory to life,
she sees the plunging weapon is a knife.

The Loft

The broken toys and fading photographs
will gather dust inside the eaves above;
the history of life falls into cracks—
some memories remain in hearts with love.

Disturbing dust that's settled on the past,
encourages a wave of tears to flood;
the speedy clock that scampered on so fast,
reflecting on a moment we misjudged.

Regret can linger on those artefacts
and gnaw at bones and infiltrate the mind;
the losses and the joys along the tracks,
as memories can sometimes be unkind.

The store of ancient echoes gather grime,
they're captured in a capsule of our time.

The Pendulum Dropped

He spoke for those who could no longer speak,
as justice will prevail beyond the grave;
and those who kill the innocent, are weak
the cowards who were never ever brave.

When persecuting others they were flawed,
whatever they maintain, it is not right;
and consequences will be our reward,
forever they will see the long cold night.

And swing they did, this band of evil men,
who found the Devil, and took tea with him;
and now recorded with my well inked pen—
how they did not believe it was a sin.

And history regurgitates with bile,
this horrid tale of Genocide, hostile.

This is a tribute to Ben Ferencz (War Crimes Prosecutor) 1920-2023, died aged 103 on 7th April 2023. A man who believed in the Law of Peace and tried men in Germany for Genocide after the war. An admiral man who at the age of 27 succeeded in convicting many men for these war crimes. None of them were remorseful.

He Said:

"If these men be immune, then the law has no meaning, and man must live in fear".

Time to Leave

Shall I move mountains, clear the sky of cloud,
make sunny days forever just for you;
and shout your name from roof tops very loud—
will this encourage love to filter though?

And from the midnight sky I'll pluck a star
and ask the moon to stay full for a week;
a choir of birds will sing just where you are
each morning will be magical, unique.

Alas, no matter what is gifted here,
the silence will remain, you have no words;
your eyes contain a frost that has no cheer,
the atmosphere is dead, and it disturbs.

I think it's time to leave and find some peace,
as staying here will give me no release.

Titan Sub

We seek adventure, risking life and limb,
regrets are only visible to others;
for they will feel the loss, their lives now dim—
the boundaries were pushed, the grief now smothers.

As life was thrown so needlessly away,
as foolishly the gamble was too high;
and those who dice with deadly death's ballet,
will have no chance to wave their last goodbye.

Regret will ring a bell in grief's long fight
to come to terms with yesterday's decision;
and nothing changes what has come to light,
as history is now a ghostly vision.

And souls are laid to rest in oceans deep,
another wreck forever is asleep.

A catastrophic implosion took place in 2023, when the Titan submersible hit the deep-sea as the water pressure crushed the vessel with 5 men on board. It would have instantaneously destroyed the ship and its occupants.

Today's Society

It's hard to slow a world that moves too fast,
to find a silent hour, a lonely road;
when satellites up in the sky are vast—
and man cannot escape the overload.

No longer do we forage, plant the seeds,
and tend the cattle, wash without machines;
our laziness encourages fatigues,
depressive thoughts now govern our routines.

In modern homes we can be isolated,
and live our days without the need to leave;
if someone calls, our home feels violated,
cocooned inside malaise they're left to grieve.

Some die of loneliness, with broken hearts,
the pace of life outside is full of sharks.

Travels in Time

There is no bitterness when I look back
I've few regrets, and life has been so good;
around the world some cases I've unpacked—
in places where I never felt secured.

From Devil's Island to the Russian Kremlin,
Manaus to Gibraltar, I've observed;
and every place has left a tiny gremlin
that itches to be bold, as some disturbed.

My travels took me to the Golden Coast,
to Bali where the beaches were so clean;
the planet has so many treasured ghosts—
remaining in my memory unseen.

But in my heart I'll always love my home,
as England is engraved upon my bone.

Tyrannical Leadership

A serpent's tongue can cut just like a knife,
as memories prevail on celluloid,
and deep within, the scar remains for life,
recurring with a voice that's paranoid.

Remembering a time that goes back years,
misguided words of anger flew about,
and caught by young and sinless eager ears
delivered in a mean and heartless spout.

Now looking back at those who held a grudge,
now dead and gone and rotting in their graves,
I wonder if regret would be their judge—
and if they knew their victims are still slaves.

Would empathy bring tears of sorrow too—
or are they just too evil to be true.

Ungrateful Child

Ungrateful is this child, she knows no strife—
there is a cruel divisive world outside,
and yet her tongue is sharper than a knife,
her thanklessness is full of foolish pride.

Insensitive to privilege and honour,
she bites the hand that feeds her love again;
behaviour of the guiltless is improper,
as naive youth knows only to complain.

Reality may dawn, we know not when,
the tantrums and the selfishness will fade;
and peace will soon return to life again,
and she will then forget her big crusade.

As ignorance will stain the bitter clout,
until the tide begins to turn about.

Unpredictability

Beware the wasp his sting can hurt a lot,
but never blame him for his actions here;
as this is his defence, he's not a clot
he will not sting if you refuse to scare.

Beware the dog he has a nasty bite,
but he would rather lick than show his teeth;
and if you stand upon his tale, he'll fight
anxiety for him is only brief.

The human can be unpredictable,
you never know if he is true or false;
we learn to trust, but hearts are fallible,
and cracks appear increasing every pulse.

We learn to navigate the human brain—
adjusting our behaviour keeps us sane.

Venom Pollutes

A drop of venom poisons with its feed
before the ink has dried and stained for good
consider some alternatives at speed,
as permanence destroys the sisterhood.

And once the tongue unleashes without care
it spreads like fire among the congregation;
and whips up quite a stormy lightning flare,
that sparks a multi-layered conversation.

Just like the Genie, once he has come out
he fights incarceration, won't lie down;
we learn the truth, and we will have no doubt,
the scorn is scandalous all over town.

Before infecting ponds with verbal slaughter,
remember others also drink the water.

Victoria Coach Station – London

The time is almost nine, I wait in line—
the frowns in town wound down by endless travel;
the sinner's eye is on the edge of crime,
and I can't wait to leave the city gravel.

My purse is strapped on tight, my case at hand,
the queue is long, and anger may erupt;
I board the bus, my seat is in demand,
and everyone around appears corrupt.

The clock it chimes, it is now nine, I ride,
I leave the grime, the crime, the slime, I smile;
and watch the pretty lights of London pride,
and leave the city rime, to tour the mile.

Victoria is cold, I'm on my guard,
the station is where many have been scarred.

Violent Threats

When anger fills the veins with red hot blood,
there is no stopping fire from rising up;
and when the spill of temper's in a flood
the threat is wild, outrageous and abrupt.

The rage is blind and frighteningly vi'lent,
and there's no compromising with the mad;
inside there is a fury that is silent,
intentions are so meaningfully bad.

Intimidation never wins the day,
it only fuels the fire, ignites the flame;
and words are empty, actions on display,
as those who act this way are filled with shame.

And those who threaten violence should know
brutality will turn on them and blow.

Wallowing in Grace

I wallow in the timelessness of grace
when viewing flowers in my summer park;
the colourful array on every face
that greets me when sun rises with the lark.

I bathe within the fluttering of leaves
that gently rustle, tease with melody;
and birds with optimistic song believe
that they will have success with family.

And I can sleep with ease in times of trouble
as what will be will be, there's no control
as someone will attempt to burst my bubble,
with courage I alone will be consoled.

I draw my strength from pretty scenes in nature,
to quell the storms ahead from my creator.

What Easter Means to Me

A time of great reflection and deep faith,
of sacrifice, forgiving those who harm;
remembering the choice we have to make
a difference on earth within a psalm.

The joy of giving, lending without gain,
to learn the lessons from that ancient book;
to make a change and start a new campaign,
and recognise the good, not overlook.

As Easter dedicates our hearts to life,
to see the error in our human flaws;
and every time we find ourselves in strife
we'll gain the strength to open other doors.

The teachings of our faith will soothe our soul,
engage our hearts and minds to keep us whole.

What Makes a Man a Man?

Is strength and courage— masculinity,
do signs of power crush his inner fears?
Are punches thrown to save his dignity?
Suppressing his emotions and his tears.

To influence all others with a scheme,
as ego rules the soul and heart within;
to be a man, does it require a dream,
to conquer, be a King, and always win?

A man to me is sensitive and kind,
and happy to come down to earth, be meek—
to open up his heart, show his true mind,
as fear is part of every working week.

And showing vulnerability is human,
a superhero is a fake illusion.

Winds Blew Hard

The wind blew high and upside down it threw
my house into a spin until it landed
upon its roof, the contents broke in two—
why was the wind so very heavy handed?

Now walking on the ceiling in my house
and stepping over chandeliers and chairs
my bedclothes strewn about, there is a mouse
confused and climbing backwards up the stairs!

I need a crane to help me flip it round
so that the loose foundations reconnect;
and I can put my feet back on the ground
before the wind disrupted and upswept.

I used to take my little home for granted—
then winds blew hard, dismantled and adapted.

Winning Ways

I see the summer living in her eyes
the ice may form, but she will melt the cold;
such warmth exudes, she always has the prize—
her presence has the power to be bold.

The magic of her smile can touch your heart,
and it will miss a beat when she is near;
she fascinates me with her special art,
reducing me to shed a little tear.

Her eyes of blue will view the world outside,
and every scene is filled with floral blooms;
her innocence can never be denied,
the air she breathes is full of sweet perfumes.

Her kindness knows no bounds, her heart is true,
she brings delight to me and all of you.

Worry Worms

Will worry ever leave our mind at rest,
as we prioritise— to fight the fire;
so many obstacles, we can protest,
anxiety will not let us retire.

There's always trouble churning inside you—
relaxing is the privilege of babes;
accepting change is something that we do,
more difficult it is with mounting age.

Remember every path we take is worn—
as others have been there, and know our pain;
decisions made may leave us weak and torn,
but rainbows colour skies behind the rain.

Imagine life without a future plight—
how boring life would be without a fight.

Wounds of War

The wounds of war go deep, they reach the bone,
they fester with revenge, and may not heal;
the truth revealed will turn some hearts to stone—
from ashes anger rises with new zeal.

For yesterday the loss was never counted,
historic reasons "why" still moan with pain;
unfinished is the battle, we're surrounded
by irksome rage within the stormy rain.

Can we forgive the past and live in peace,
let venomous emotion spoil our day?
Can we forget and find some sweet release,
and let recrimination slip away?

Alas the past is littered with those ghosts,
who left behind their vengeful anecdotes.

Write a Sonnet

When sonnet writing headlines in the news—
and everyone is keen to write their best;
our mindful focus wakes our inner muse,
and all our skill is then put to the test.

The metre and the stresses are in place,
and we have found a story worthy too—
our words are edged with power and with grace,
we pen with ink that's bold and wise and true.

But one thing to remember when we write,
critique comes from a personal perspective
and we may never reach— or show the light-
to someone who can never be reflective.

So let your sonnet shine, write from the heart,
you'll never know success, until you start.

The Author's Biography

Christine was born in Birmingham, in the United Kingdom, where she has spent most of her life. Her passion and love of poetry started at college when she was lucky enough to have her first poem published, 'The Beach', at the age of seventeen. Since then she has developed her talent for rhyming words, and many more poems have been published on 'Amazon', 'Forward Poetry' and 'The United Press'. Her poems have also won contests on Fanstory.com. She is pleased to present another book called: Spirited Sonnets.

Other recent poetry books include:

'300 Soulful Sonnets		300 traditional Shakespearean Sonnets
'Naughty Limericks		A full colour illustrated book
'Glimpsing Light in Poetry'	-	500 Poems with b/w illustrations
101 Poetic Personalities from History		A full colour book of famous faces
'A Plethora of Poignant Poetry'	-	200 Poems with b/w illustrations
'The Fascinating World of POETIC Bugs "	-	100 Poems with full colour illustrations
'The Poetic Philosophy of Life'	-	130 Poems with b/w illustrations
'POETIC Bird Watch'	-	A full colour book of birds
'POETIC Flowering Blossom'	-	A full colour book of flowers
'Nature's Poetic Chimes'	-	A full colour nature book
'The Awdl Sonnet'	-	Dedicated to the Awdl Sonnet form

All available on Amazon.com

She originally worked as an aerobics fitness instructor for local authority gyms around Birmingham, and also Aston University, before retiring.

The inspiration for this book comes from personal experiences of love and loss, emotions, reflections and challenges in daily life. The influence of nature on our world and environment is profound and our inner peace and calm is the result of good thoughts and a positive attitude. Admiration and appreciation for others, including wildlife, enhances one's feeling of well-being. The joys of life are free, if we just open our eyes to them. My muse is the pleasure in life itself, the power to survive is strong in all creatures on earth.

Welcome to: "Spirited Sonnets"

Write for Posterity

A word, it never ages over time,
and from conception it remains in youth;
as fresh as daisies, each and every rhyme,
has roots inside a moment of great truth.

In future years, those words will tell a tale,
just like a photograph, the clock will stop;
and captured is important rare detail—
the history that poems can unlock.

Remember what you see today will fall
into the archives of our distant past,
when sentiment is penned, albeit small,
it evidences time that's built to last.

So write those words and use your skilful art,
as future folk will take them to their heart.

MMXXIII

Spirited Sonnets

Poems by Christine Burrows

Printed in Great Britain
by Amazon

32685676R00099